Muhlenberg County Libraries
108 E. Broad St.
Central City, Kentucky 42230

DATE DUE

W9-DAA-643

SUPER SIMPLE

CLASSIC

cookies

EASY COOKIE RECIPES FOR KIDS!

ALEX KUSKOWSKI

Consulting Editor, Diane Craig, M.A./Reading Specialist

Super Sandcastle

An Imprint of Abdo Publishing
abdopublishing.com

JN
CC 0508
$18.95
8/17

abdopublishing.com

Published by Abdo Publishing, a division of ABDO, PO Box 398166, Minneapolis, Minnesota 55439. Copyright © 2016 by Abdo Consulting Group, Inc. International copyrights reserved in all countries. No part of this book may be reproduced in any form without written permission from the publisher. Super SandCastle™ is a trademark and logo of Abdo Publishing.

Printed in the United States of America, North Mankato, Minnesota
102015
012016

THIS BOOK CONTAINS RECYCLED MATERIALS

Editor: Liz Salzmann
Content Developer: Nancy Tuminelly
Cover and Interior Design and Production: Mighty Media, Inc.
Photo Credits: Mighty Media, Inc., Shutterstock

The following manufacturers/names appearing in this book are trademarks:
Arm & Hammer®, C&H®, Calumet®, Crisco®, Market Pantry™, McCormick®, Philadelphia®, Proctor Silex®, Roundy's®

Library of Congress Cataloging-in-Publication Data
Kuskowski, Alex, author.
Super simple classic cookies : easy cookie recipes for kids! / Alex Kuskowski.
   pages cm. -- (Super simple cookies)
ISBN 978-1-62403-947-8
1. Cookies--Juvenile literature. 2. Baking--Juvenile literature. I. Title.
TX772.K775 2016
641.86'54--dc23
                    2015020592

Super SandCastle™ books are created by a team of professional educators, reading specialists, and content developers around five essential components—phonemic awareness, phonics, vocabulary, text comprehension, and fluency—to assist young readers as they develop reading skills and strategies and increase their general knowledge. All books are written, reviewed, and leveled for guided reading and early reading intervention programs for use in shared, guided, and independent reading and writing activities to support a balanced approach to literacy instruction.

TO ADULT HELPERS

Help your child learn to cook! Cooking lets children practice math and science. It teaches kids about responsibility and boosts their confidence. Plus they get to make some great food!

Before getting started, set ground rules for using the kitchen, cooking tools, and ingredients. There should always be adult supervision when use of a sharp tool, oven, or stove is required. Be aware of the symbols below that indicate when special care is necessary.

So, put on your apron and get ready to cheer on your new chef!

SYMBOLS

Hot!
This recipe requires the use of a stove or oven. You will need adult supervision and assistance.

Sharp!
This recipe includes the use of a sharp utensil such as a knife or grater. Ask an adult to help out.

Nuts!
This recipe includes nuts. Find out whether anyone you are serving has a nut allergy.

CONTENTS

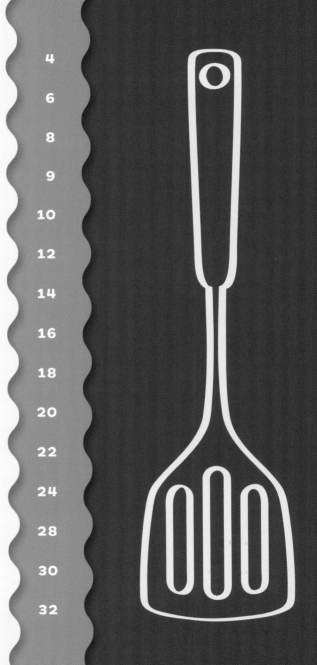

Time to Go Cookie Crazy   4

Cooking Basics   6

Measuring Ingredients   8

Did You Know This = That?   9

Cooking Terms   10

Kitchen Utensils   12

Ingredients   14

Classic Chocolate Chip   16

Chewy Oat Cookies   18

Sugar Drops   20

Peanut Butter Cookies   22

Chocolate & Cream Sandwiches   24

Sweet & Soft Snickerdoodles   28

Butterscotch Delights   30

Glossary   32

TIME TO GO COOKIE CRAZY

Classic cookies are a sure bet for a hit. You'll want to make them again and again. They make a **delicious** treat any time!

The classic cookie **recipes** in this book are super simple. Cooking teaches you about food, measuring, and following directions. And you get to have delicious cookies! Share your tasty creations with family and friends.

 # COOKING BASICS

Think Safety!

- Ask an adult to help you use a knife. Place things on a cutting board to cut them.

- Clean up spills right away.

- Keep things away from the edge of the table or **counter**.

- Ask an adult to help you use the oven.

- Ask for help if you cannot reach something.

Using the Oven

- Preheat the oven while making the **recipe**.

- Use oven-safe dishes.

- Use pot holders or oven mitts to hold hot things.

- Do not touch the oven door. It can be very hot.

- Set a timer. Check the food and bake longer if needed.

Before Baking

- Get **permission** from an adult.

- Wash your hands.

- Read the recipe at least once.

- Set out the ingredients and tools you will need.

- Keep a **towel** close by for cleaning up spills.

When You're Done

- Let the cookies cool completely.

- Store the cookies in **containers**. Put a sheet of waxed paper in between the **layers** of cookies.

- Put all the ingredients and tools away.

- Wash all the dishes and **utensils**. Clean up your work space.

MEASURING INGREDIENTS

Wet Ingredients

Set a measuring cup on the **counter**. Add the liquid. Stop when it reaches the amount you need. Check the measurement from eye level.

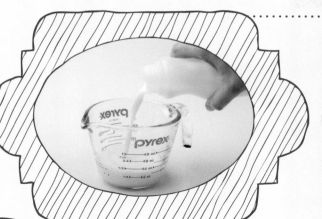

Dry Ingredients

Dip the measuring cup or spoon into the dry ingredient. Fill it with a little more than you need. Use the back of a dinner knife to remove the extra.

Moist Ingredients

Measure ingredients such as brown sugar and dried fruit differently. Press them down into the measuring cup.

DID YOU KNOW THIS = THAT?

There are different ways to measure the same amount.

3 teaspoons = 1 tablespoon

4 tablespoons = ¼ cup

5 tablespoons + 1 teaspoon = ⅓ cup

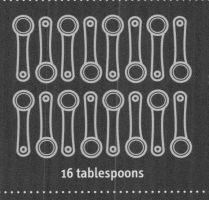

16 tablespoons = 1 cup

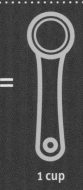

1 cup

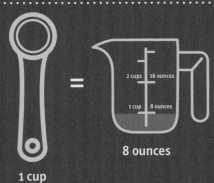

1 cup = 8 ounces

2 cups — 16 ounces
1 cup — 8 ounces

1 stick of butter = ½ cup

2 cups — 16 ounces
1 cup — 8 ounces

2 cups = 1 pint

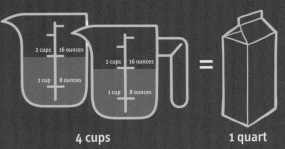

2 cups — 16 ounces
1 cup — 8 ounces

2 cups — 16 ounces
1 cup — 8 ounces

4 cups = 1 quart

2 quarts = ½ gallon

COOKING TERMS

CREAM

Cream means to beat butter and sugar together until light and **fluffy**.

STIR

Stir means to mix ingredients together, usually with a spoon or rubber spatula.

BEAT

Beat means to mix well using
a whisk or electric mixer.

SPREAD

Spread means to make a smooth **layer**
with a spoon, knife, or rubber spatula.

KITCHEN UTENSILS

spoon

fork

measuring spoons

measuring cups

cookie cutters

baking sheet

electric mixer

cutting board

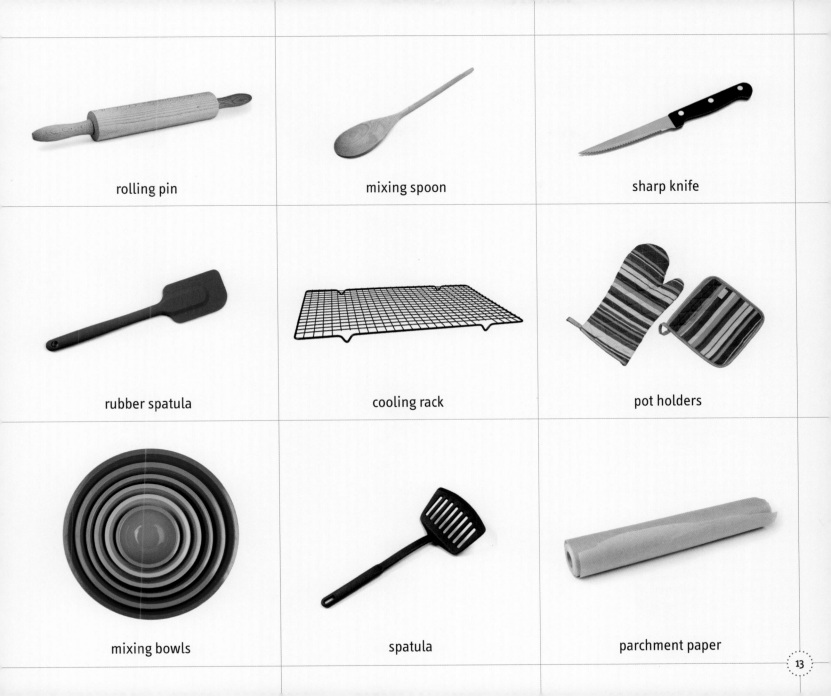

rolling pin

mixing spoon

sharp knife

rubber spatula

cooling rack

pot holders

mixing bowls

spatula

parchment paper

INGREDIENTS

all-purpose flour

almond extract

baking powder

baking soda

brown sugar

butter and unsalted butter

butterscotch chips

chopped walnuts

cream cheese

cream of tartar

crunchy peanut butter

eggs

ground cinnamon

milk

old-fashioned oats

powdered sugar

salt

semi-sweet chocolate chips

shortening

unsweetened cocoa powder

vanilla extract

white sugar

15

classic
chocolate
chip

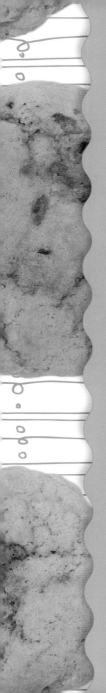

MAKES 30 COOKIES

INGREDIENTS

2 cups all-purpose flour
1 teaspoon salt
1 teaspoon baking soda
1 cup butter
½ cup white sugar
1 cup brown sugar
1 teaspoon vanilla extract
2 eggs
2 cups semi-sweet
   chocolate chips

· · · · · · · · · · · · · · · ·

TOOLS

baking sheets
parchment paper
measuring cups
measuring spoons
mixing bowls
electric mixer
rubber spatula
spoon
pot holders
spatula
cooling rack

1 Preheat the oven to 350 degrees.
   Cover the baking sheets with
   parchment paper.

2 Put the flour, salt, and baking
   soda in a medium bowl. Stir them
   together. Set the bowl aside.

3 Put the butter, white sugar, and
   brown sugar in a separate bowl. Beat
   with a mixer for 3 minutes. Beat in
   the vanilla and eggs.

4 Add the flour mixture to the butter
   mixture. Add it 1 cup at a time. Beat
   the ingredients together after each
   cup. Add the chocolate chips 1 cup at
   a time. Stir after each cup.

5 Use a spoonful of dough for each
   cookie. Place them on the baking
   sheet 2 inches (5 cm) apart.

6 Bake for 10 minutes or until they are
   golden brown. Put the cookies on a
   cooling rack.

chewy
oat
cookies

MAKES 30 COOKIES

INGREDIENTS

¾ cup shortening

½ cup white sugar

1¼ cups brown sugar

2 tablespoons vanilla
    extract

1 egg

⅓ cup milk

3 cups old-fashioned oats

1 cup all-purpose flour

½ teaspoon baking soda

½ teaspoon salt

½ teaspoon ground
    cinnamon

1 cup semi-sweet
    chocolate chips

1 cup chopped walnuts

· · · · · · · · · · · · · · · · · ·

TOOLS

baking sheets

parchment paper

measuring cups

measuring spoons

mixing bowls

electric mixer

mixing spoon

rubber spatula

spoon

pot holders

spatula

cooling rack

1 Preheat the oven to 375 degrees.
   Cover the baking sheets with
   parchment paper.

2 Put the shortening, sugars, vanilla,
   egg, and milk in a medium bowl.
   Beat them together.

3 Put the oats, flour, baking soda, salt,
   and cinnamon in a large bowl. Stir
   them together.

4 Add the shortening mixture to the
   oats mixture. Stir the ingredients
   together. Stir in the chocolate chips
   and walnuts.

5 Use a spoonful of dough for each
   cookie. Place them on the baking
   sheet 2 inches (5 cm) apart.

6 Bake for 12 minutes. Put the cookies
   on a cooling rack.

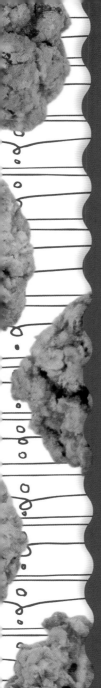

sugar drops

MAKES 20-30 COOKIES

INGREDIENTS

3 cups all-purpose flour
1 teaspoon baking soda
½ teaspoon salt
1 cup butter
2 cups white sugar
2 eggs
1 teaspoon almond extract
1 teaspoon vanilla extract

. . . .

TOOLS

baking sheets
parchment paper
measuring cups
measuring spoons
mixing bowls
mixing spoon
electric mixer
spoon
pot holders
spatula
cooling rack

1 Preheat the oven to 350 degrees. Cover the baking sheets with parchment paper.

2 Put the flour, baking soda, and salt in a large bowl. Stir them together.

3 Put the butter and 1¾ cups sugar in a separate large bowl. Beat for 1 minute. Beat in the eggs, almond extract, and vanilla.

4 Add the flour mixture to the butter mixture. Beat them together.

5 Use a spoonful of dough for each cookie. Place them on the baking sheet 2 inches (5 cm) apart. Sprinkle some of the remaining sugar on top of each cookie.

6 Bake for 15 minutes. Put the cookies on a cooling rack.

peanut
butter
cookies

INGREDIENTS

3 cups all-purpose flour

1½ teaspoons baking soda

1 teaspoon baking powder

½ teaspoon salt

1 cup unsalted butter

1 cup white sugar

1 cup brown sugar

2 eggs

1 teaspoon vanilla extract

1½ cups crunchy peanut butter

. . . .

TOOLS

baking sheets

parchment paper

measuring cups

measuring spoons

mixing bowls

mixing spoon

electric mixer

rubber spatula

spoon

fork

pot holders

spatula

cooling rack

1. Preheat the oven to 375 degrees. Cover the baking sheets with parchment paper.

2. Put the flour, baking soda, baking powder, and salt in a medium bowl. Stir them together.

3. Cream the butter and sugar in a large bowl. Beat in the eggs and vanilla.

4. Add the flour mixture to the butter mixture. Beat the ingredients together. Stir in the peanut butter.

5. Use a spoonful of dough for each cookie. Place them on the baking sheet 2 inches (5 cm) apart. Flatten each cookie in two directions with a fork.

6. Bake for 10 minutes or until they are light brown. Put the cookies on a cooling rack.

chocolate & cream sandwiches

INGREDIENTS

COOKIES

1¼ cups all-purpose flour

½ cup unsweetened cocoa powder

½ teaspoon baking soda

¼ teaspoon baking powder

¼ teaspoon salt

1 egg

1 cup unsalted butter

1 cup white sugar

FILLING

8 ounces cream cheese

4 tablespoons unsalted butter

2 cups powdered sugar

2 teaspoons vanilla extract

. . . .

TOOLS

baking sheets

parchment paper

measuring cups

measuring spoons

mixing bowls

mixing spoon

electric mixer

rolling pin

cookie cutter

pot holders

spatula

cooling rack

spoon

1. Preheat the oven to 350 degrees. Cover the baking sheets with parchment paper.

2. Put the flour, cocoa, baking soda, baking powder, and salt in a medium bowl. Stir them together.

3. Put the egg, butter, and sugar in a large bowl. Beat them together.

4. Add the flour mixture to the egg mixture. Beat the ingredients together.

5 Lay two sheets of parchment paper on the **counter**. Sprinkle them with flour. **Divide** the dough in half. Put each half on a sheet of parchment paper. Sprinkle flour on the dough.

6 Put flour on the rolling pin. Roll each dough half to ¼ inch (0.6 cm) thick.

7 Put the dough in the refrigerator for 30 minutes.

8 Cut out cookies with a cookie cutter. Place them on the baking sheet 1 inch (2.5 cm) apart. Reroll the dough to cut out more cookies.

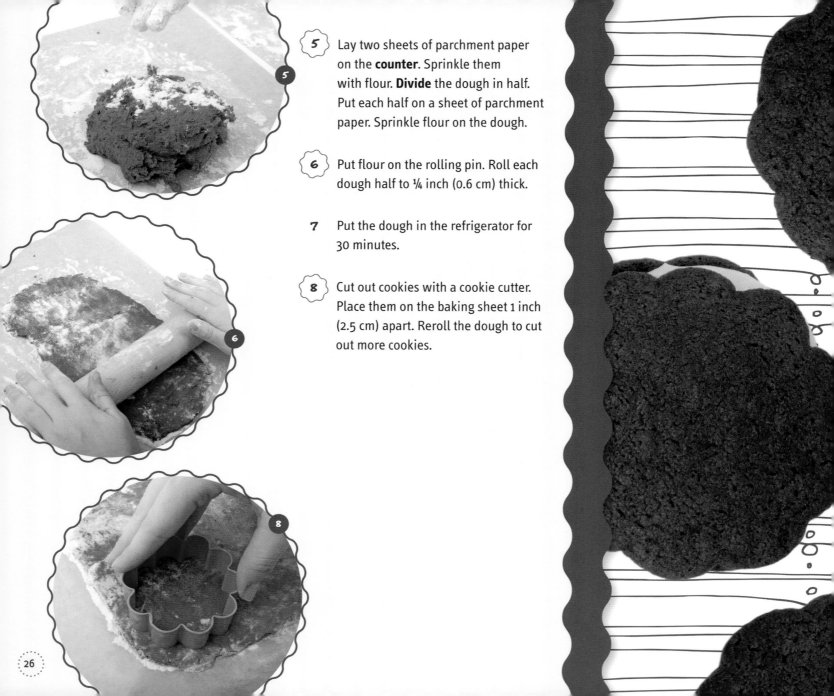

9 Bake 10 minutes. Put the cookies on a cooling rack. Let them cool 5 minutes.

10 Put the filling ingredients in a bowl. Beat them together.

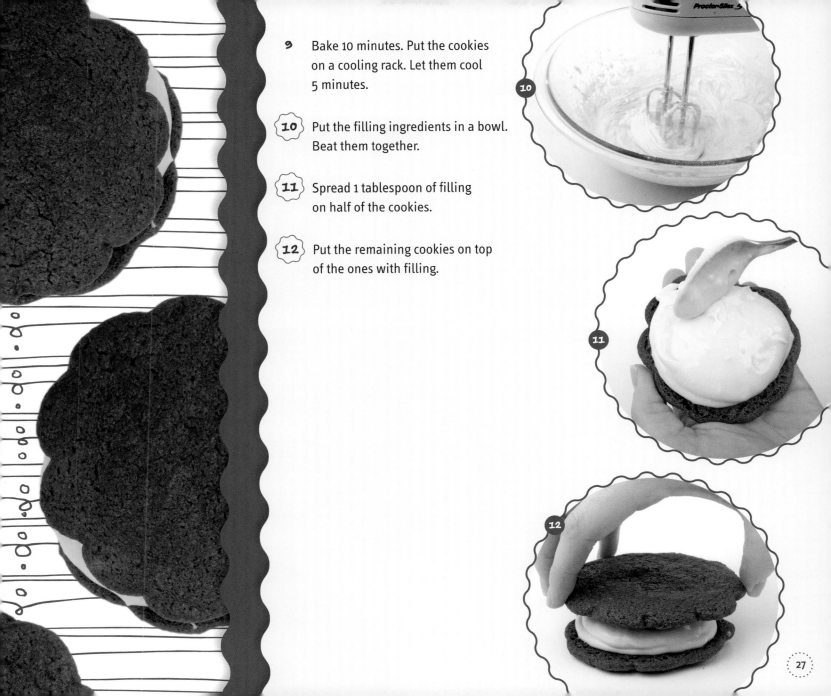

11 Spread 1 tablespoon of filling on half of the cookies.

12 Put the remaining cookies on top of the ones with filling.

sweet & soft snickerdoodles

INGREDIENTS

1 cup unsalted butter

1½ cups white sugar

2 eggs

1 teaspoon vanilla extract

2¾ cups all-purpose flour

2 teaspoons cream of tartar

1 teaspoon baking soda

½ teaspoon salt

4 tablespoons brown sugar

3 teaspoons ground cinnamon

. . . .

TOOLS

baking sheets

parchment paper

measuring cups

measuring spoons

mixing bowls

electric mixer

mixing spoon

whisk

pot holders

spatula

cooling rack

1 Preheat the oven to 350 degrees. Cover the baking sheets with parchment paper.

2 Put the butter, white sugar, eggs, and vanilla in a large bowl. Beat them together.

3 Put the flour, cream of tartar, baking soda, and salt in a medium bowl. Stir them together. Add the flour mixture to the butter mixture. Beat the ingredients together. Put the dough in the refrigerator for 15 minutes.

4 Put the brown sugar and cinnamon in a small bowl. Stir them together.

5 Roll the dough into 1-inch (2.5 cm) balls. Roll each cookie ball in the sugar mixture. Place them on the baking sheet 2 inches (5 cm) apart.

6 Bake 12 to 15 minutes or until light brown. Put the cookies on a cooling rack.

butterscotch delights

INGREDIENTS

1 cup unsalted butter

1¼ cups brown sugar

1 egg

2 teaspoons vanilla
   extract

1½ cups all-purpose flour

½ teaspoon salt

½ teaspoon baking soda

½ cup butterscotch chips

. . . .

TOOLS

baking sheets

parchment paper

measuring cups

measuring spoons

mixing bowls

electric mixer

mixing spoon

rolling pin

sharp knife

cutting board

pot holders

spatula

cooling rack

1 Preheat the oven to 350 degrees.
   Cover the baking sheets with
   parchment paper.

2 Cream the butter and sugar
   in a large bowl. Beat in the egg
   and vanilla.

3 Put the flour, salt, and baking soda
   in a medium bowl. Stir them together.
   Add the flour mixture to the butter mixture.
   Beat the ingredients together. Beat in the
   butterscotch chips.

4 Lay out a sheet of parchment paper. Sprinkle
   it with flour. Put the dough on the parchment
   paper. Cover the rolling pin with flour. Roll the
   dough into a rectangle ¼ inch (0.6 cm) thick.

5 Starting at a short end, roll the dough into a
   log. Wrap it in the parchment paper. Put the
   dough in the refrigerator for 30 minutes.

6 Cut the log into ¼-inch (0.6 cm) **slices**.
   Place them on the baking sheet
   2 inches (5 cm) apart.

7 Bake for 10 minutes or until they
   are light brown. Put the cookies
   on a cooling rack.

GLOSSARY

container – something that other things can be put into.

counter – a level surface where food is made.

delicious – very pleasing to taste or smell.

divide – to separate into equal groups or parts.

fluffy – light, soft, and airy.

layer – one thickness of something that may be over or under another thickness.

permission – when a person in charge says it is okay to do something.

recipe – instructions for making something.

slice – a thin piece cut from something.

towel – a cloth or paper used for cleaning or drying.

utensil – a tool used to prepare or eat food.

Muhlenberg County Libraries
108 E. Broad St.
Central City, Kentucky 42230